I've had dogs all my life. My parents had four generations of poodles in the 50s and 60s. Once the 70s arrived they naturally moved on to Afghan hounds – Casanis and Ottoline, a mother and daughter who were beautiful, wayward and none too bright. Following them came Battersea, an apparently charming mongrel who regularly bit my mother when nobody was looking. They finally reverted back to poodles with Bognor, a beautiful, silly, apricot standard. Inexplicably, they then moved onto cats.

I took over the family dog ownership with Fanny, a dogs' home mongrel with big hair, like an extra member of Duran Duran. She had a huge personality and firm views. Then came Dorothy, a Dalmatian, who was sweet natured and loved everyone. At the same time we accidentally acquired Jack Swan – the most beautiful golden greyhound found wandering the streets of Bath. I said I'd look after him for the weekend... we had him for one short year before he died in his sleep. Following Jack Swan came two whippets: devoted Lily, who is always by my side, and Peggy, slightly less devoted and always in a patch of sun.

For almost as long as I have had dogs I have drawn and painted them and mine star multiple times in this book. Several years ago I began a simple Facebook project, 'A Dog a Day', posting my dog art daily. Some days I drew or painted several pieces, some days I didn't do any, but every day I posted a new one. As people became interested, I became more adventurous in my materials. Wire drawing, lithography, paper cuts, pen and ink, and potato prints are among the media I tried out, to keep both myself and my kind followers interested. Although the project finished several years ago, I still post dog pictures regularly.

Through 'A Dog a Day' I found my perfect job. I find people and their dogs endlessly fascinating. I love how devoted people and dogs are to each other, how dogs have such distinct personalities and how we attribute complex emotions to them. Dogs bring out the best, and sometimes the worst, in people. I try to interpret each dog as the individual that he or she is. I take creating a dog portrait as seriously as I do a human portrait. I do like people as well, it's not an either/or thing, but I could very happily paint or draw a dog a day for the rest of my life.

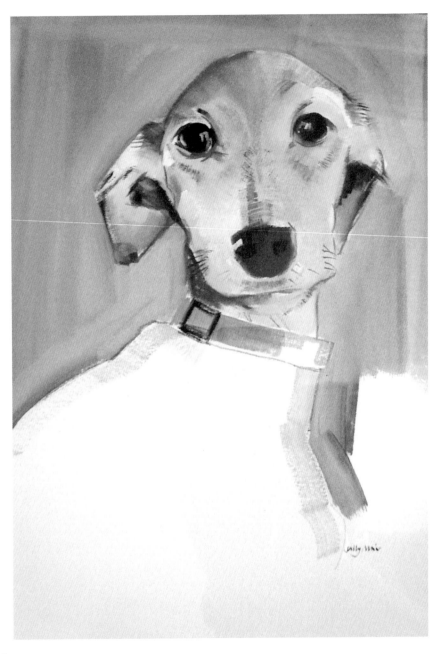

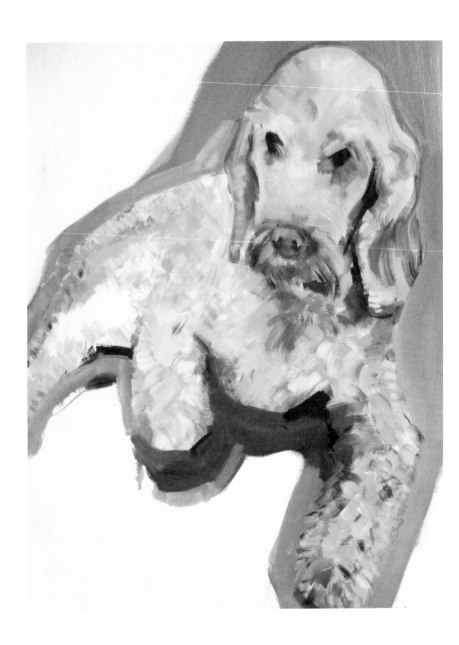

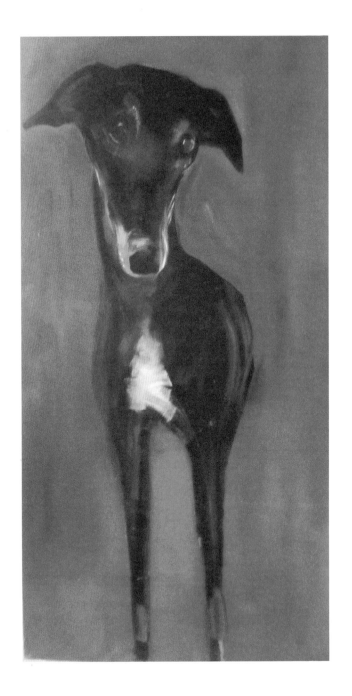

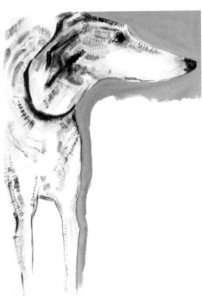

45

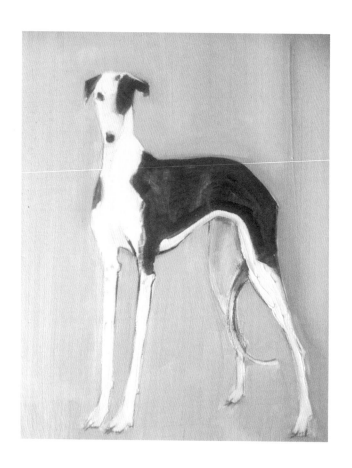

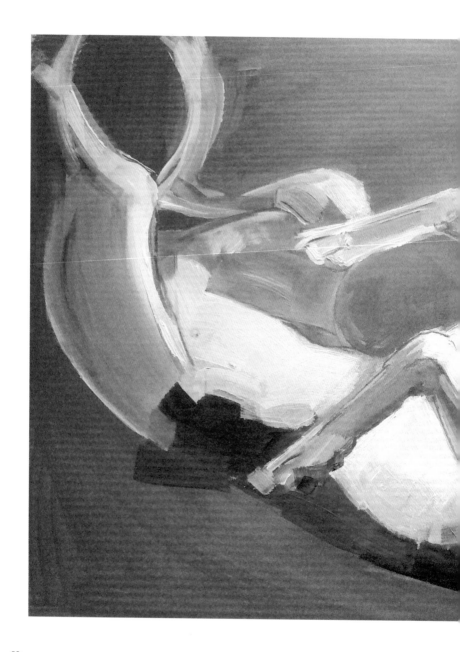

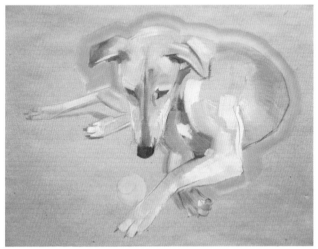

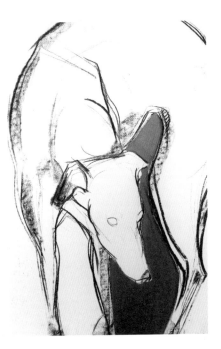

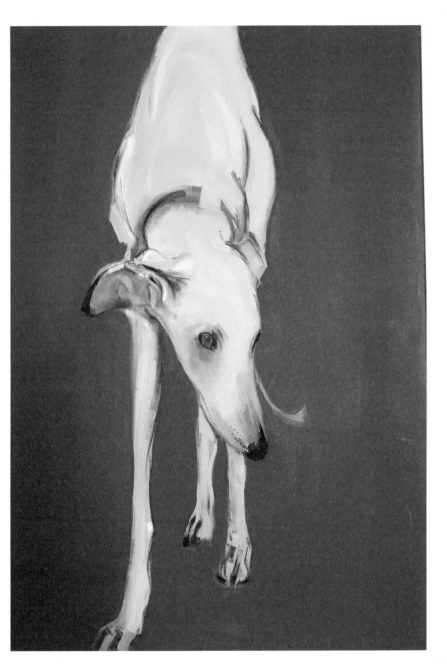

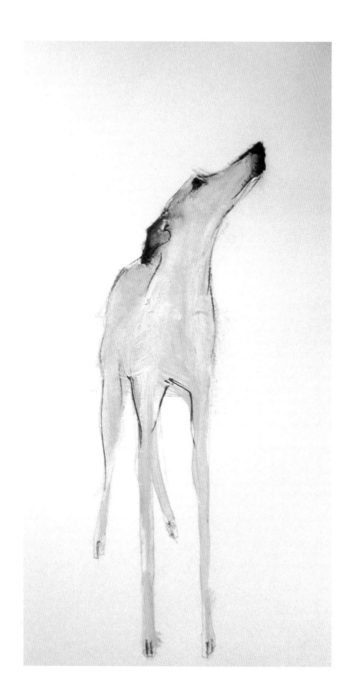

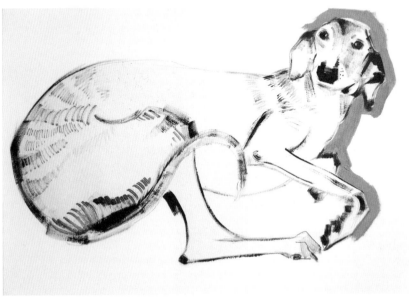

117

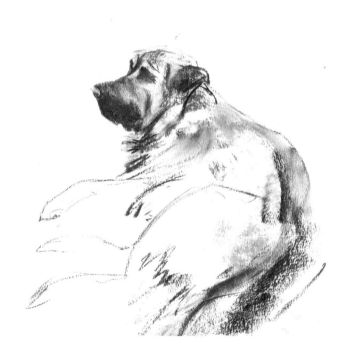

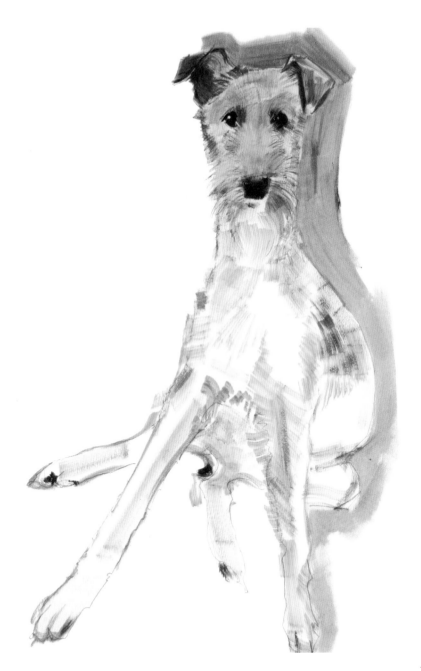

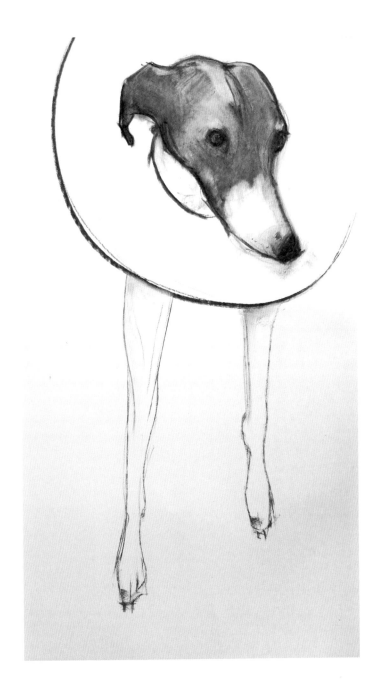

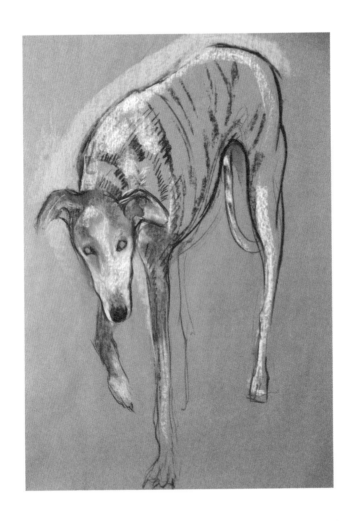

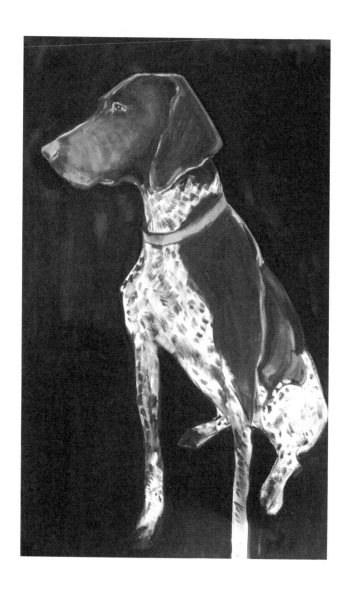

158

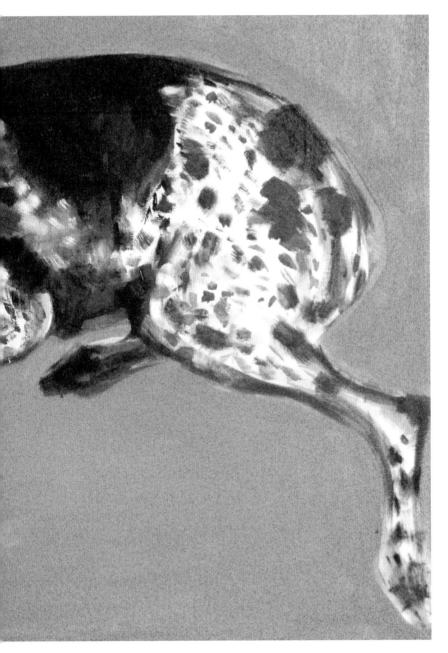

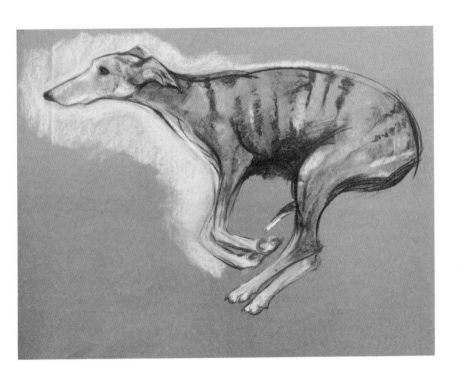

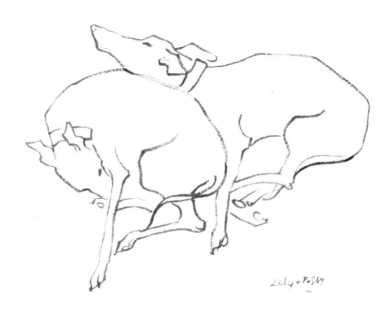

Lily + Poppy

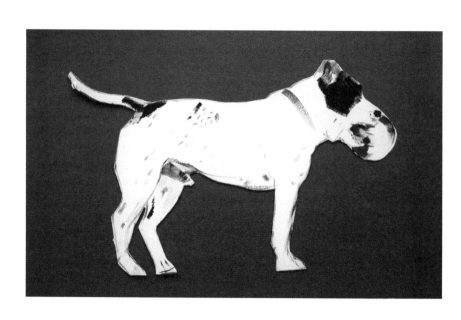

186

194

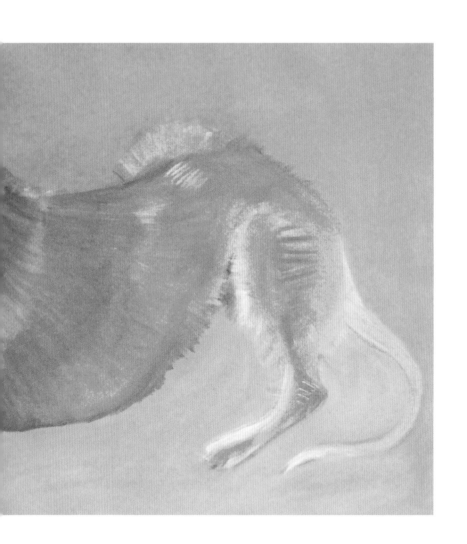

236

1. Ronnie, pen and ink
2. Dorothy, oil on board
5. Multiple Galgos, oil on paper
6. Galgo, oil on paper
7. Bradley, oil on board
8. Multi vertical line dogs, pen and ink
9. Piper, pastel
10. Golden dog, oil on paper
11. Imaginary hound, oil on board
12. Lurcher puppy, BCDH, oil on paper
13. Henry, oil on board
14. Lurcher, BCDH, oil on paper
15. Nellie, oil on paper
16. Simon, charcoal and gouache
17. Whopper, charcoal and gouache
18. Edie, oil on board
19. Maddie, oil on paper
20. Purdey, oil on paper
21. Pumpkin, oil on board
22. Lily, oil on paper
23. Roger, oil on paper
24. Granny Pants, GDS, oil on paper
25. Hound, oil on board
26. Galgo, oil on board
27. Connie, oil on board
28. George, oil on paper
29. Penny, oil on board
30. Imaginary dachshund, oil on board
32. Timber and Dudley, oil on board
32. Lily and Luna, oil on board
33. Hans, oil on board
34. Galgo, oil on paper
35. Jimmy, oil on board
36. Rosie, Boo and Tegan, potato print
37. Jet, charcoal and gouache
38. Whippet puppy, charcoal
39. Bear, oil on paper
40. Imaginary dog, oil on paper
41. Japanese Chin, charcoal
42. Rambo, oil on board
43. Naked dog, oil on canvas
44. Hairy Galgo, oil on board
45. Galgo puppy, oil on board
45. Brindle Galgo, oil on paper
46. Jack Swan, pen and ink
46. Peggy, pen and ink
47. Watson, oil on paper
48. Be, oil on canvas
49. Charity, GDS, oil on paper
50. Greyhound, oil on board
51. Greyhound, oil on board
52. Lily rolling, oil on paper
54. Luna, oil on paper
55. Jack Swan, oil on paper
56. Imaginary scribble dog, biro
57. Lorax, oil on paper

57. Maggie, oil on paper
58. Molly, oil on paper
59. Perdita, oil on board
60. Ludo, oil on board
60. Rita, pastel
61. Hound, pen and ink
61. Poppy, charcoal
61. Buttercup, charcoal
61. Scratching dog, lithograph
62. Imaginary lurcher, charcoal and gouache
63. Bichon, oil on paper
63. Freddy, oil on board
64. Plum, charcoal
65. Staffie in the street, oil on paper
65. Lurcher, BCDH, oil on paper
66. Bull terrier, potato print
67. Berry, GDS, oil on paper
68. Saskia, GDS, oil on board
69. Untitled, oil on paper
70. Fifteen minute drawings, charcoal
71. Spaniel, BCDH, oil on paper
72. Rooney, oil on board
73. Whopper, charcoal
74. Scratching dog, charcoal and gouache
75. Peggy, iPhone
75. Hound, charcoal and gouache
76. Hound, charcoal
77. Sarah's terrier, oil on paper
78. Galgo, oil on paper
79. Inky, charcoal
80. Dog outside shop, monoprint
80. Dog outside shop, monoprint
81. Galgo, oil on canvas
82. Hound, pen and ink and wash
83. Sugar, oil on board
84. Lily, oil on paper
85. Wire haired dachshund, oil on canvas
86. Staffie, BCDH, oil on paper
87. Dusty, charcoal
87. Dorothy, graphite
88. Pug, Galgo, Galgo, potato prints
89. Poppy and Slipper, oil on paper
90. Keiko, oil on paper
91. Wire haired dachshund, oil on board
91. Roy, oil on board
92. Imaginary lurcher, oil on paper
93. Dee, oil on board
94. Hound, charcoal
94. Duncan, oil on board
95. Rosi, oil on paper
96. Keiko, charcoal
97. Brodie, oil on board

98. Hound, pen and ink
98. Pete, lighograph
99. Fuzzface, GDS, pastel
100. Granny Pants, GDS, oil on paper
101. Billie, oil on paper
102. Holly, oil on board
104. Lurcher puppy, BDCH, oil on board
105. Brodie, oil on paper
106. Declan, GDS, oil on paper
107. Scribble dog, lithograph
108. Priscilla Queen of the Dachshunds, oil on board
109. Galgo, GDS, oil on board
110. Cosmo and Percy, oil on board
111. Maisie and Pete, oil on board
112. Imaginary hairy dog, oil on paper
113. Dusty, charcoal and pastel
114. George, oil on canvas
115. Staffie type, BCDH, oil on paper
115. Gordon, oil on paper
116. Daisy, oil on board
117. Perdita, oil on canvas
117. Lincoln, oil on canvas
118. Lurcher, BCDH, oil on paper
119. Lula, oil on paper
120. Lily and Peggy, iPad
122. Lola, watercolour
122. Lucy, pastel and gouache
122. Lurcher, BCDH, oil on paper
122. Brucie, BCDH, oil on paper
123. Pug, oil on board
124. Benji, pastel
125. Daphne, pastel
125. Stella, pastel
126. Buttercup, lithograph
127. Columbo, oil on paper
128. Brigitte, oil on paper
129. Galgo, GDS, oil on paper
130. Bess, oil on board
131. Untitled, oil on board
132. Sidney, oil on canvas
133. Chutney, oil on paper
134. Staffie puppy, BCDH, oil on paper
135. Untitled, oil on paper
136. Harold, GDS, charcoal
137. Martha, oil on paper
138. Noah, oil on board
139. Dorothy, oil on board
140. Untitled, oil on paper
141. Lily in cone, charcoal
142. Multi hound, potato print
143. Gracie, oil on canvas
144. Blind and deaf dog, BCDH, oil on paper
145. Galgo, GDS, pastel and gouache

Thank you to all the dogs who have modelled and to all their owners too. I have tried my very best to remember all their names, please forgive me if I have forgotten them. Also thank you to Bath Cats and Dogs Home and Galgos del Sol, who have let me roam around and draw and photograph their dogs. Thank you to Pavilion for suggesting this book and for making it so lovely. Particular thanks to Caitlin who had the unenviable job of counting to make sure that there are actually 365 dogs.

First published in the United Kingdom in 2017 by
Pavilion
43 Great Ormond Street
London
WC1N 3HZ

Copyright © Pavilion Books Company Ltd 2017
Text and image copyright © Sally Muir 2017

ISBN 978-1-91121-691-9

A CIP catalogue record for this book is available
from the British Library.

10 9 8 7 6 5 4 3 2

Reproduction by
Mission Productions Ltd, Hong Kong

Printed and bound by GPS Group, Slovenia

This book can be ordered direct from the publisher
at www.pavilionbooks.com